Hustle Culture Workbook

K.A. Perkins

Published by: G & P Unlimited Co. L.L.C.
K. A. Perkins
Dayton, Ohio 45406
ISBN:978-1-7369074-1-2
Copyright 2020 by K.A. Perkins
All rights reserved.

In whole or in part without the author's written consent, the Reproduction of the text is not permitted and unlawful according to the 1976 United States Copyright Act. Printed and distributed by G&P Unlimited Co. LLC.

G & P UNLTD. CO. INTERACTIVE

At G & P Unlimited Co., we are excited to offer our branded series of Interactive books. Interactive books are used to help you, the reader, to organize and learn the information covered in this book. The reasoning behind creating interactive books originated with actual research-based classroom instructional strategies like notetaking, concept mapping, and organizing information to assist your learning. G&P Unlimited Interactive books' goal combines all this research into one instructional method to promote your education. We do this through charts, infographics, *visualizations, and journaling.*

We purposefully designed this book to be larger so that you can use the margins and open spaces to draw, doodle, cartoons, create personalized wording of vocabulary, and document inspired thought. So, write in the book, color, and draw. Make this book your learning masterpiece; what you will discover as you engage with our Interactive Book/ Activities to tools that will empower your life. Remember to carry your markers!

Share your masterpiece! We are creators just like you, and we would love to see your interpretation of what you have learned and your engagement with this interactive book. Please email us at info@gpunltd.com or use hashtag #GPINTERACTIVE.

SECTION I: The Dilemma

1. What drives you to want to be successful?

   _____
   _____
   _____
   _____
   _____

2. What are the three things you need to be successful?

   a. S_____

   b. C_____

   c. P_____

3. Why do you think so many people lack the necessary skills, principles, and competencies that are needed to succeed?

   _____
   _____
   _____
   _____
   _____

4. How do you handle failures, disappointments, and growth moments?

   _____
   _____
   _____
   _____
   _____

5. **Do you think your dreams are a reflection of something deeper within your mind?**

   Explain

   _____
   _____
   _____
   _____
   _____

6. **In your own words, define the following:**
   - Determination:
   _____
   - Hard Work:
   _____
   - Resiliency:
   _____

7. **How would you describe the current season of your life? What are your current opportunities and challenges?**

   _____
   _____
   _____
   _____
   _____
   _____
   _____

8. **Research the type of career or job that you want to have and identify some skills that that you need to be successful.**

   _____
   _____
   _____
   _____
   _____
   _____

9. **Why do you think employers feel that it is essential for future employees to be problem-solvers, collaborators, leaders, and managers of their own careers?**

   _____
   _____
   _____
   _____
   _____

10. **Activity-** *For the next four weeks, start your day 30 minutes earlier. Use that 30 minutes to process your day and set priorities. You will find that you will get more done and save time when investing at least an additional 30 minutes to your day.*

    Summarize Your Results

    _____
    _____
    _____
    _____
    _____

SECTION II: Leaving Grind to Find Hustle

1. In your own words, define Grind.

_____
_____
_____
_____
_____
_____
_____

2. In your own words, define Hustle.

_____
_____
_____
_____
_____
_____
_____

3. Define Grind Mentality.

_____
_____
_____
_____
_____
_____
_____

4. **Define Hustle Culture.**

   _____
   _____
   _____
   _____

5. **In your own words, what are the six components that combine to make Hustle Culture?**

   a. _____
   b. _____
   c. _____
   d. _____
   e. _____
   f. _____

6. **Fill in the blank:**
   Hustle Culture will take

   _____
   _____
   _____
   _____
   _____

7. **What does HCHM stand for?**

   _____

8. **What is the ideal version of yourself you want to be? Explain**

   _____
   _____
   _____
   _____

9. **In your own words explain the importance of the following:**
   - Skill-

   _____
   _____

- Education-
  _____

- Work Ethic-
  _____

- Ambition-
  _____

- Mental Muscle-
  _____

10. **Activity-** *Spend the next four weeks planning your day the night before you If your actually write a to-do list while you plan, it will help you get better sleep.*

Summarize Your Results

_____
_____
_____
_____
_____
_____
_____
_____
_____
_____
_____
_____
_____
_____

SECTION III-Welcome Hustle Culture

1. In the diagram below, differentiate between Hustle and Grind?

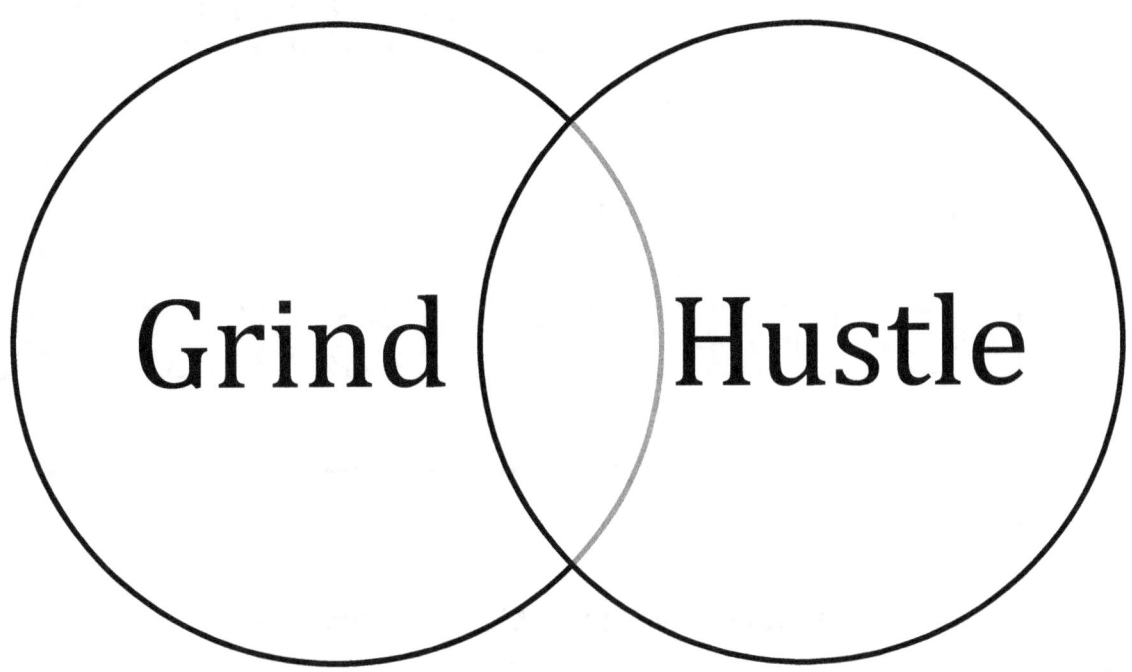

2. A niche market means that your product, service, talent, and skill are tailored to satisfy the need of a targeted demographic. In the space below identify your niche:

_____
_____
_____
_____
_____
_____
_____
_____

3. Fill in Formula for Success

V+W+F+L+C=S

_____+_____+_____+_____+_____=_____

4. Fill in Formula for Hustle Culture

HC (INPUT)=SFC (OUTPUT)

_____=_____

5. Fill-In components of Hustle Culture Formula

(SK+C+P)(S)=H

_____+_____+_____ X _____=HUSTLE

6. In the space below explain why time is a commodity.

_____
_____
_____

7. Identify the ten symptoms of grinding?

- _____
- _____
- _____
- _____

- _____
- _____
- _____
- _____
- _____
- _____

8. Respond to the following two questions?
   A. *What is the reality you wish for yourself?*

   _____
   _____
   _____
   _____
   _____
   _____
   _____

   B. *How does your ideal reality compare to your current reality?*

   _____
   _____
   _____
   _____
   _____
   _____
   _____
   _____

9. Explain how your career aligns with your goals.

   _____
   _____
   _____
   _____
   _____
   _____
   _____

10. **Activities- Do your most creative work in the morning.** *For the next four weeks start doing the task that requires creativity or detail early in the morning. It is in the morning that your body uses cortisol chemicals to help you focus and maintain concentration. Use the afternoon for more simpler tasks.*

Summarize your results below.

SECTION IV: Hustle Culture Paradigm Shift

1. How close are you to achieving your big dreams?

A. What do you see as obstacles in your path towards your dream?

2. Why do you think rich folks don't teach Hustle Culture rules?

3. What is the difference between a laborer and an owner?

4. Workforce and personal survival and stainability in the next 50 years will be based on your ability to be:

   A. _____
   B. _____
   C. _____
   D. _____
   E. _____
   F. _____
   G. _____

5. Hustle Culture Success is finding out what your purpose is in life, then educating yourself and developing the Skills, Competencies, and Principles needed to fulfill that purpose. How do you define your purpose?

   _____
   _____
   _____
   _____
   _____
   _____
   _____

6. Write the six-fold purpose of education.

   1. _____
      _____

   2. _____
      _____

   3. _____
      _____

4. _____
   _____

5. _____
   _____

6. _____
   _____

7. **Fill in the formula for Hustle Culture Champion**

   # G+I=HCC

   _____ + _____ = _____

8. **I this section of the manual, we spent a lot of time discussing the purpose of education. Your belief about education is the foundation for your life philosophy. In the space below summarize your personal belief about education.**

   _____
   _____
   _____
   _____
   _____
   _____
   _____
   _____
   _____

SECTION V-Skills, Competencies, and Principals

1. Work Ethic- Fill in the spaces in the chart.

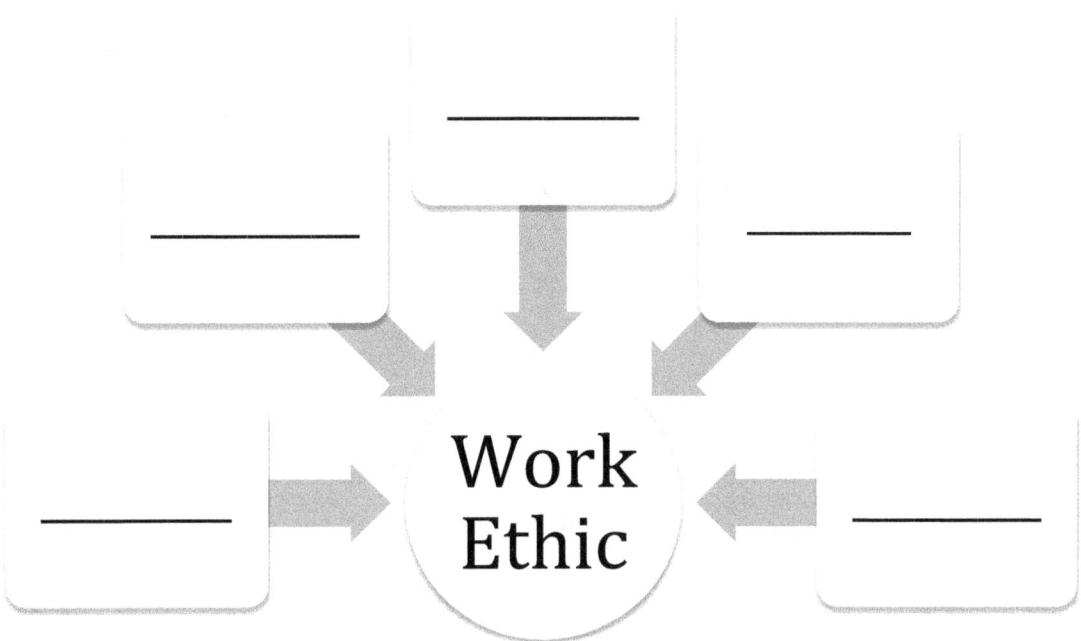

2. In the space below assess your level of focus and your plan to improve.

_____
_____
_____
_____
_____
_____
_____

3. What is your plan to eliminate distractions?

_____
_____
_____
_____
_____

4. How will you focus on one thing?

_____
_____
_____
_____
_____
_____

5. Create a daily plan with dedicated time for focused work.

_____
_____
_____
_____

6. What are some options you can use to increase your focus?

_____
_____

_____
_____
_____
_____

7. What personal strengths help you to work more efficiently?

_____
_____
_____
_____
_____
_____

8. What steps can you take to be more punctual in your Hustle efforts?

_____
_____
_____
_____
_____
_____

9. What is your definition of professionalism?

_____
_____
_____

_____
_____
_____
_____
_____

10. What steps can you take to develop a work-life balance?

_____
_____
_____
_____
_____

11. Fill in the chart for soft skills:

Soft Skills

_____
_____
_____
_____
_____
_____
_____
_____
_____
_____
_____
_____
_____
_____

12. Fill in the chart of Effective Communication Skills:

_____	_____	_____	_____
_____	_____	_____	_____
	_____	_____	

13. In your own words, summarize emotional intelligence.

_____
_____
_____
_____
_____
_____

14. In your own words, summarize active listening.

_____
_____
_____
_____
_____
_____

15. In your own words, summarize non-verbal communication.

_____
_____
_____

16. In your own words, summarize clarity.

_____
_____
_____
_____
_____
_____
_____

17. In your own words, explain summarizing as it relates to communication.

_____
_____
_____

18. How does empathy improve communication?

_____
_____
_____

19. How would you give feedback?

_____
_____
_____
_____

20. How does trust and rapport improve communication?

_____

21. When having a conversation, what does it mean to be present?

_____

_____

_____

22. What is industry writing?

_____

_____

_____

23. Fill in the Chart for Workplace Relationships and Demeanor

Do	Do Not
_____	_____
_____	_____
_____	_____
_____	_____
_____	_____

24. What are some important rules for phone and voicemail etiquette?

_____

_____

_____

25. Identify one important consideration when writing an email?

_____
_____
_____

26. What are some things that you should not do when you are using a work computer?

_____
_____
_____

27. Give me an example of excellent customer service?

_____
_____
_____

28. What are the ten simple rules of fantastic customer service?

- _____
- _____
- _____
- _____
- _____
- _____

- _____
- _____
- _____
- _____

29. Why are employers willing to pay more for creative individuals?

_____
_____
_____
_____
_____

30. Identify 5 ways to improve your organization?

- _____
- _____
- _____
- _____
- _____

31. What are 5 tools that you can use to improve your time management?

- _____

- _____
- _____
- _____
- _____

32. Identify 5 practices to incorporate when you are networking?

- _____
- _____
- _____
- _____
- _____

33. Please Circle the Correct Answers (Professional Appearance)

a. **Which of the following is the best example of professional business dress?**
   - Otis is wearing blue dress pants with a nice, collared shirt and vest to match.
   - Kelly is wearing a black skirt suit with two-inch heels.
   - Travis is wearing khaki pants and a nice polo.
   - Nyla is wearing jeans with a nice blouse and suit jacket.

b. **Which of the following is the best example of business casual?**
   - Otis wearing khaki pants and a t-shirt.
   - Nyla is wearing jeans with a nice blouse and suit jacket.
   - Travis is wearing black dress pants with a nice, collared shirt and vest to match.
   - Kelly is wearing a navy skirt suit with two-inch heels.

c. **Which of the following colors is NOT considered as appropriate for a business dress suit?**
- navy
- green
- gray
- black

d. **6-inch heels are appropriate attire for business dress as long as the woman can walk in them comfortably.**
- True
- False

e. **A proper handshake has which four elements?**
- sweaty hands, firm grip, eye contact, smile
- dirty hands, firm grip, eyes on hands, smile
- dirty hands, crushing grip, eye contact, smile
- clean hands, firm grip, eye contact, smile

f. **How does your professional appearance impact your career?**
- Your appearance does not affect your career.
- As long as you have a strong resume, your appearance never matters.
- Your appearance only impacts your career if you are in the business sector.
- Your appearance strongly influences other people's perception of your suitability for hire or promotion.

g. **Your clothing should always be stylish and_____.**

- Functional
- Formal
- Highly accessorized
- Colorful
- Expensive

34. In the boxes provided draw and label the table setting.

Draw and Label Basic Table Setting

Draw and Label Informal Table Setting

Draw and Label Formal Table Setting

Draw and Label Multi-Course Table Setting

35. Choose the correct answer:

   a. When you have finished eating, place the knife and fork _____.
   - On the plate
   - Neither on the plate or the table

- In your drinking glass
- On the table

b. Begin to eat_____.
- As soon as you are seated
- When everyone has been served
- When the everyone is served, and the host starts eating.
- When you are served

c. Sit comfortably at the table, with your feet_____.
- On the chair
- Around the chair
- On the floor
- Stretched under the table

d. What adds MOST to the enjoyment of a meal?
- Expensive food
- Decorations
- Conversation
- Lots of good tasting food

e. It is proper to_____.
- Talk with your lips full of food
- Pass Gas at the table
- Chew with your mouth open
- Burb
- Chew with your mouth closed

f. When drinking water, hold the glass_____.
- With a straw with the glass on the table
- Around the rim
- With both hands
- Near the base

g. When you are eating, keep_____.
- The elbows on the table
- The elbows off the table

- One elbow on the table

h. What should you do when food you dislike is served to you?
- Tell the host that is nasty
- Take it off your plate
- Eat everything else and do not eat the food that you dislike

i. When bread is served at the meal_____.
- Break off a small piece and butter it
- Cut piece in half and butter it
- Butter a whole piece at a time

j. When you have finished eating_____.
- Put your elbows on the table
- Push your plate to one side
- Leave your plate in place
- Push your plate back

36. Identify 4 examples of personal integrity?
  A. _____
  B. _____
  C. _____
  D. _____

37. Summarize what it means to be flexible and adaptable.

_____
_____
_____
_____
_____
_____
_____
_____
_____
_____

38. What does it mean to be independent and self-motivated?

39. Give an example of when you were reliable and responsible.

40. What in an example of a great leader?

_____

_____

_____

_____

_____

41. Complete and Professionalism Quiz

A. TRUE/FALSE

____Keeping nails neatly trimmed and clean only applies to women not to men.

____All professionals display professionalism at all times.

B. Multiple Choice

Would any company culture encourage upper-level management to wear Hawaiian shorts and polo shirts to work?

- Yes
- No

C. Identify 5 examples of successful work propensities.

- _____
- _____
- _____
- _____
- _____

42. Explain in your own words Career Management

_____

_____

_____

_____

_____

_____

_____

43. Define Global/Intercultural Fluency.

_____

_____

_____

_____

44. Fill in the verbal communication chart and summarize what you learned.

Verbal Communication

___ ___ ___ ___

   a. List 5 communication tools for leadership:

_____
_____
_____
_____
_____
_____
_____
_____

   b. What should effective communication with clients be focused on?

_____
_____
_____
_____
_____
_____
_____
_____
_____
_____
_____
_____
_____
_____

_____
_____
_____
_____
_____
_____
_____
_____
_____

45. Fill in the written Communication chart and summarize what you learned.

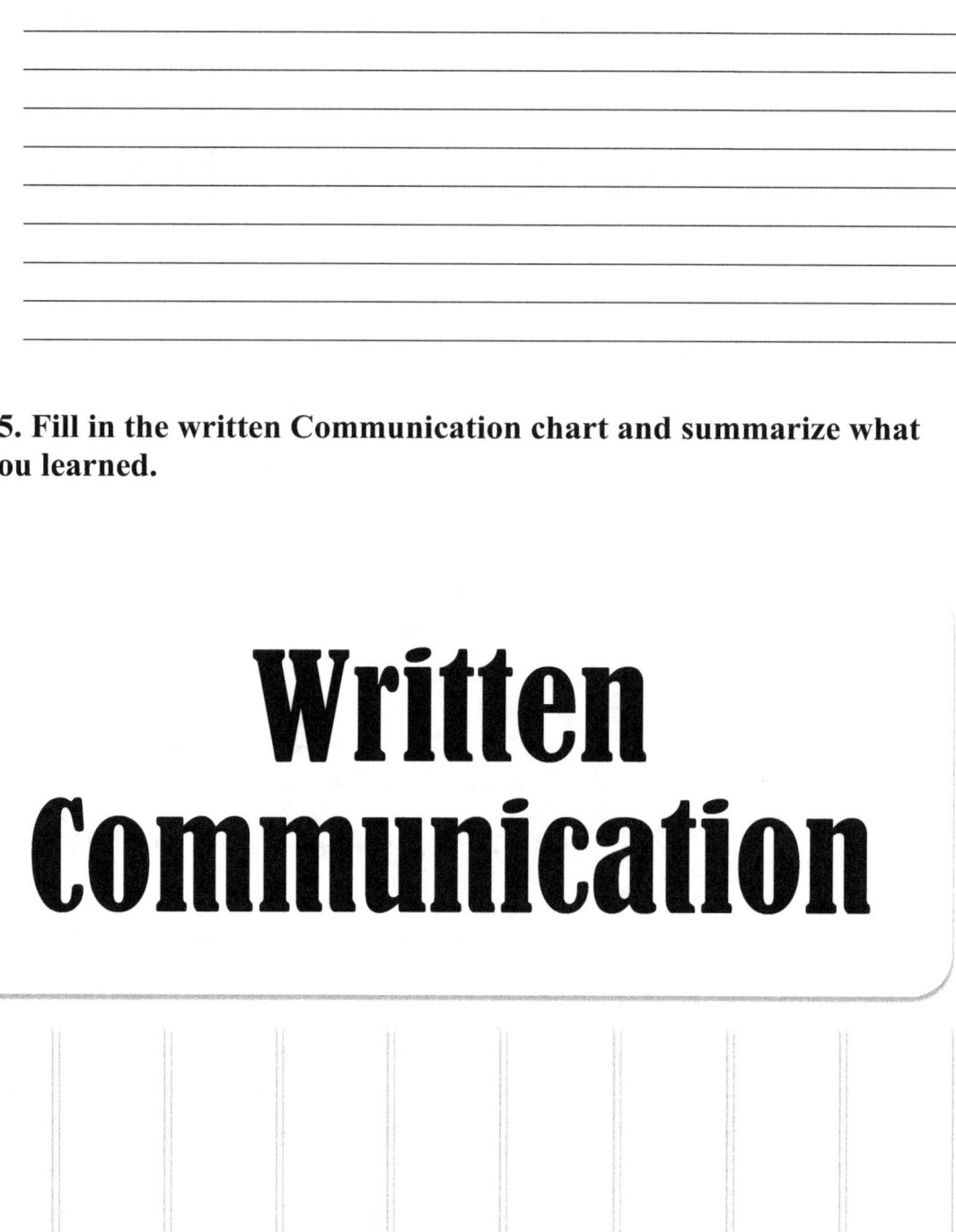

a. Summarize what you have learned about written communication?

_____
_____
_____
_____
_____

b. Identify 3 tips you want to incorporate in your written communication.

_____
_____
_____
_____

46. Define and give an example of teamwork.

_____
_____
_____
_____
_____
_____
_____
_____
_____
_____

47. Based on the leadership chart in the book, what is your leadership style?

_____
_____
_____
_____

48. Why is it important to have research skills?

_____
_____
_____
_____
_____
_____
_____
_____

49. In your own word, summarize assimilating data.

_____
_____
_____

50. How does data interpretation work in the workforce?

_____
_____
_____
_____

51. What are some things that you can do to be an effective problem solver?

_____
_____
_____
_____
_____
_____
_____

Pillar 2-Hustle Culture Competencies

1. Fill in the chart below:

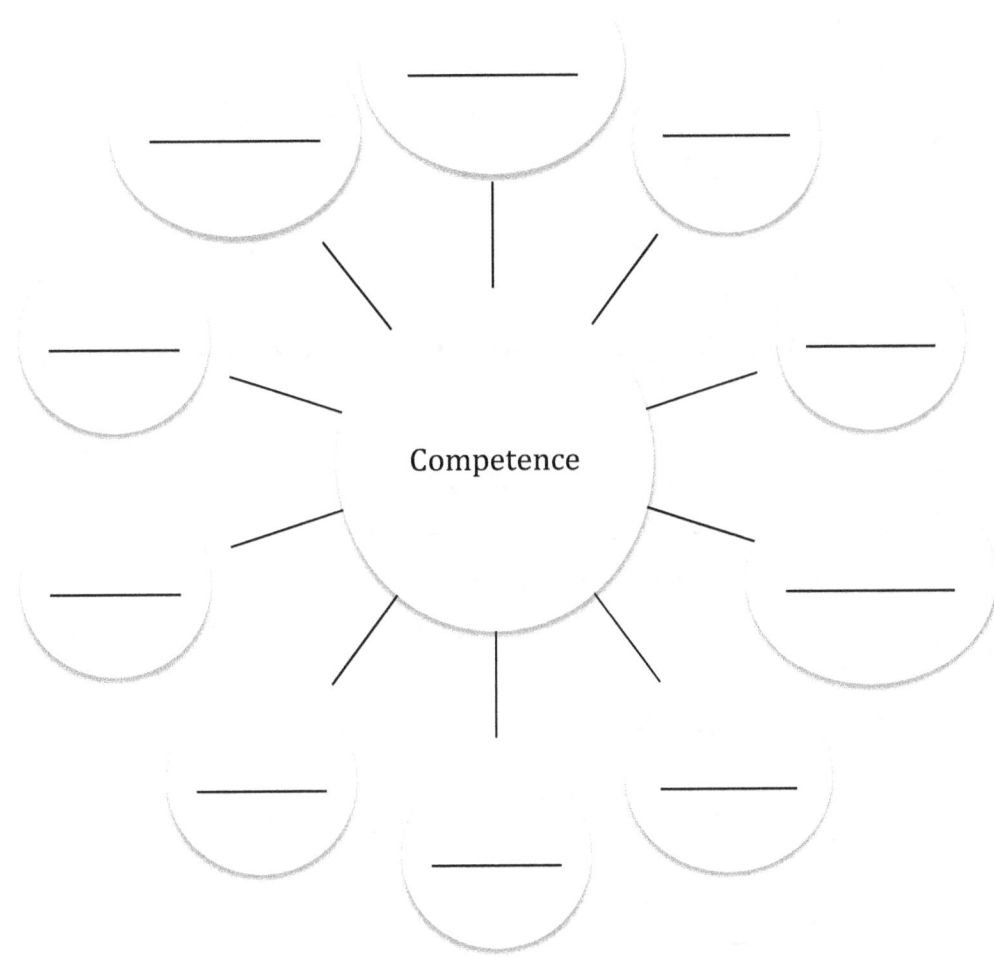

2. **Base on the chart on Technological Competence, what are the competencies of which you currently have a working knowledge?**

   A. _____
   B. _____
   C. _____
   D. _____

1. What are the ten things that you can do to increase Cultural Competence?

   - _____
   - _____
   - _____
   - _____
   - _____
   - _____
   - _____
   - _____
   - _____
   - _____

3. What are five things that you can do to improve your Global Competence?

   - _____
   - _____
   - _____
   - _____
   - _____

4. In what ways are you Environmentally Competent?

   _____
   _____
   _____
   _____
   _____
   _____
   _____
   _____
   _____

5. In what ways will you demonstrate Political and Civic Competence?

   _____
   _____

_____
_____

6. **What are some keywords and/or phrases that when used, will showcase your Industry/ Corporate Competence?**

    - _____
    - _____
    - _____
    - _____
    - _____

7. **List the ten essential basics of Financial Competence:**

    - _____
    - _____
    - _____
    - _____
    - _____
    - _____
    - _____
    - _____
    - _____
    - _____

8. **Summarize your understanding of Entrepreneurship Competence.**

    _____
    _____
    _____
    _____

9. **Explain Personal Branding and what it means to you.**

    _____
    _____
    _____
    _____

10. **How can you improve your Self-Maintenance?**

    _____
    _____
    _____

Pillar 3-Hustle Culture Principles

1. **Reflect on how you will release your Pearls of Possibility?**

2. **Why do hustlers only fellowship with other Hustlers?**

3. **Why is it important to always have Tikvah?**

4. **What does it mean to have a spirit of excellence, and what does it look like in your life?**

5. For what do you have faith to drown?

6. Reflect on what it means to "Chill Out, Be Amazing, Be In-Control".

7. What are the three things you can do to unleash your self-awareness?
   -
   -
   -

8. Since it is never too late; what is one thing that you want to go after?

9. Why is it important to take risk?

10. What does "Everyday Must Count" mean?

11. Write at least five rules of loyalty.

12. How does changing your mind change your life?

13. What are two things that you can do to develop productive habits?

14. What does collaborating with others look like?

15. Reflect on what it means to have an "Can't Stop, Won't Stop Mentality".

16. What are your willing to fight for when it comes to your personal and professional development?

17. What is your interpretation of a Healthy Lifestyle?

18. Habits - The Making or Breaking Factor Activity

- Identify three of the most important tasks needed to be completed during the day.
- Make time to work on these important tasks.
- Select organizational tools that will hold you accountable and help you create a daily plan.
- Journal and document tasks that are completed.

Do this for the next 60 days and don't stop working until you have completed the three most important tasks of the day. **Summarize your results.**

_____
_____
_____
_____
_____
_____
_____
_____
_____
_____
_____
_____
_____
_____

19. What will your life look like when you "Do You and are Epic About It"?

_____
_____
_____
_____
_____
_____
_____
_____

20. What are a few things that prevent you from soaring?

_____
_____
_____

21. Fill in the following:

Purpose Statement

Vision Statement

Value System

Mission Statement

SECTION VI: Hustle Transformation

1. **Write a plan on how you will incorporate The Law of Action Planning in your life.**

2. What is your plan to use the Law of Building to improve your personal and professional life?

3. What does the Law of Being mean to you and how will use the law to create a Hustle Culture Lifestyle?

Section VII-Assessment

Personal and Professional Development Readiness Assessment

This assessment is designed to measure your Hustle Culture personal and professional development readiness. Those who are successful tend to be more inwardly reflective, but they are also proactive in their overall self-care. Being the best is exhausting and it will push you to your limits but an individual who is successful is able to mentally adapt to situations quicker great self-care strategies, which are the foundation to your hustle culture success.

To assess your Hustle Culture Readiness, answer the following 62 questions as honest as you possibly can and tally your results at the end of the assessment.

1. Pray or meditate regularly

I do this well	I do this OK	I rarely do this	I don't do this or never thought to do it	N/A
4	3	2	1	0

2. Ask for help when I need it

I do this well	I do this OK	I rarely do this	I don't do this or never thought to do it	N/A
4	3	2	1	0

3. Regularly participate in what you enjoy

I do this well	I do this OK	I rarely do this	I don't do this or never thought to do it	N/A
4	3	2	1	0

4. Be curious and seek enrichment in life

I do this well	I do this OK	I rarely do this	I don't do this or never thought to do it	N/A
4	3	2	1	0

5. Eat healthy

I do this well	I do this OK	I rarely do this	I don't do this or never thought to do it	N/A
4	3	2	1	0

6. Act from state of Curiosity

I do this well	I do this OK	I rarely do this	I don't do this or never	N/A

			thought to do it	
4	3	2	1	0

7. Take time to chat with co-workers and friends

I do this well	I do this OK	I rarely do this	I don't do this or never thought to do it	N/A
4	3	2	1	0

8. Make time to see friends

I do this well	I do this OK	I rarely do this	I don't do this or never thought to do it	N/A
4	3	2	1	0

9. Get regular medical care for prevention (e.g., annual wellness check-ups)

I do this well	I do this OK	I rarely do this	I don't do this or never thought to do it	N/A
4	3	2	1	0

10. Openness and vulnerability with loved ones (sharing strengths, weaknesses, hopes and fears)

I do this well	I do this OK	I rarely do this	I don't do this or never thought to do it	N/A
4	3	2	1	0

11. Do something creative

I do this well	I do this OK	I rarely do this	I don't do this or never thought to do it	N/A
4	3	2	1	0

12. Make time for reflection

I do this well	I do this OK	I rarely do this	I don't do this or never thought to do it	N/A
4	3	2	1	0

13. Identify what is meaningful in my life

I do this well	I do this OK	I rarely do this	I don't do this or never thought to do it	N/A
4	3	2	1	0

14. Acknowledge your strengths

I do this well	I do this OK	I rarely do this	I don't do this or never thought to do it	N/A
4	3	2	1	0

15. Set and maintain healthy boundaries

I do this well	I do this OK	I rarely do this	I don't do this or never thought to do it	N/A
4	3	2	1	0

16. Take time to rest

I do this well	I do this OK	I rarely do this	I don't do this or never thought to do it	N/A
4	3	2	1	0

17. Do what is important to you

I do this well	I do this OK	I rarely do this	I don't do this or never thought to do it	N/A
4	3	2	1	0

18. Eat regularly (e.g., breakfast, lunch and dinner)

I do this well	I do this OK	I rarely do this	I don't do this or never thought to do it	N/A
4	3	2	1	0

19. Arrange workspace so it is comfortable and comforting

I do this well	I do this OK	I rarely do this	I don't do this or never thought to do it	N/A
4	3	2	1	0

20. Contribute to causes in which I believe

I do this well	I do this OK	I rarely do this	I don't do this or never thought to do it	N/A
4	3	2	1	0

21. Take time to journal

I do this well	I do this OK	I rarely do this	I don't do this or never thought to do it	N/A
4	3	2	1	0

22. Confront fears

I do this well	I do this OK	I rarely do this	I don't do this or never thought to do it	N/A
4	3	2	1	0

23. Stay in contact with long distance friends (more than just through Facebook)

I do this well	I do this OK	I rarely do this	I don't do this or never thought to do it	N/A
4	3	2	1	0

24. Set goals

I do this well	I do this OK	I rarely do this	I don't do this or never thought to do it	N/A
4	3	2	1	0

25. Tell my loved ones that I care for them

I do this well	I do this OK	I rarely do this	I don't do this or never thought to do it	N/A
4	3	2	1	0

26. Be opened to not knowing

I do this well	I do this OK	I rarely do this	I don't do this or never thought to do it	N/A
4	3	2	1	0

27. Exercise

I do this well	I do this OK	I rarely do this	I don't do this or never thought to do it	N/A
4	3	2	1	0

28. Find a spiritual connection or community

I do this well	I do this OK	I rarely do this	I don't do this or never thought to do it	N/A

I do this well	I do this OK	I rarely do this	I don't do this or never thought to do it	N/A
4	3	2	1	0

29. Intentionally minimize stress in my life

I do this well	I do this OK	I rarely do this	I don't do this or never thought to do it	N/A
4	3	2	1	0

30. Embrace change

I do this well	I do this OK	I rarely do this	I don't do this or never thought to do it	N/A
4	3	2	1	0

31. Laugh with others

I do this well	I do this OK	I rarely do this	I don't do this or never thought to do it	N/A
4	3	2	1	0

32. Recite affirmations

I do this well	I do this OK	I rarely do this	I don't do this or never thought to do it	N/A
4	3	2	1	0

33. Do what makes me happy

I do this well	I do this OK	I rarely do this	I don't do this or never thought to do it	N/A
4	3	2	1	0

34. Set limits with others

I do this well	I do this OK	I rarely do this	I don't do this or never thought to do it	N/A
4	3	2	1	0

35. Ask for feedback from superiors and peers

I do this well	I do this OK	I rarely do this	I don't do this or never thought to do it	N/A
4	3	2	1	0

36. Be open to inspiration

I do this well	I do this OK	I rarely do this	I don't do this or never thought to do it	N/A
4	3	2	1	0

37. Recover from disappointments and setbacks

I do this well	I do this OK	I rarely do this	I don't do this or never thought to do it	N/A
4	3	2	1	0

38. Get enough sleep

I do this well	I do this OK	I rarely do this	I don't do this or never thought to do it	N/A
4	3	2	1	0

39. Appreciate the non-material aspects of my life

I do this well	I do this OK	I rarely do this	I don't do this or never thought to do it	N/A
4	3	2	1	0

40. Spend time with my pets

I do this well	I do this OK	I rarely do this	I don't do this or never thought to do it	N/A
4	3	2	1	0

41. Take action steps to check things of a bucket list

I do this well	I do this OK	I rarely do this	I don't do this or never thought to do it	N/A
4	3	2	1	0

42. Negotiate for my needs (respect, benefits, grades, pay raise etc.)

I do this well	I do this OK	I rarely do this	I don't do this or never thought to do it	N/A
4	3	2	1	0

43. Celebrate small victories

I do this well	I do this OK	I rarely do this	I don't do this or never thought to do it	N/A

4	3	2	1	0

44. Avoid comparing self with others

I do this well	I do this OK	I rarely do this	I don't do this or never thought to do it	N/A
4	3	2	1	0

45. Allow myself to cry

I do this well	I do this OK	I rarely do this	I don't do this or never thought to do it	N/A
4	3	2	1	0

46. Learn from mistakes

I do this well	I do this OK	I rarely do this	I don't do this or never thought to do it	N/A
4	3	2	1	0

47. Schedule regular activities with my children

I do this well	I do this OK	I rarely do this	I don't do this or never thought to do it	N/A
4	3	2	1	0

48. Set Priorities

I do this well	I do this OK	I rarely do this	I don't do this or never thought to do it	N/A
4	3	2	1	0

49. Complete tasks

I do this well	I do this OK	I rarely do this	I don't do this or never thought to do it	N/A
4	3	2	1	0

50. Take breaks when feeling overwhelmed or frustrated

I do this well	I do this OK	I rarely do this	I don't do this or never thought to do it	N/A
4	3	2	1	0

51.   Seek out opportunities for self-improvement

I do this well	I do this OK	I rarely do this	I don't do this or never thought to do it	N/A
4	3	2	1	0

52.   Allow others to do things for me

I do this well	I do this OK	I rarely do this	I don't do this or never thought to do it	N/A
4	3	2	1	0

53.   Embrace challenge

I do this well	I do this OK	I rarely do this	I don't do this or never thought to do it	N/A
4	3	2	1	0

54.   Replace negative thoughts with positive thoughts

I do this well	I do this OK	I rarely do this	I don't do this or never thought to do it	N/A
4	3	2	1	0

55.   Spend time in nature

I do this well	I do this OK	I rarely do this	I don't do this or never thought to do it	N/A
4	3	2	1	0

56.   Love myself

I do this well	I do this OK	I rarely do this	I don't do this or never thought to do it	N/A
4	3	2	1	0

57.   Take breaks from cellphones, email and the internet

I do this well	I do this OK	I rarely do this	I don't do this or never thought to do it	N/A
4	3	2	1	0

58.   View disappointments and setbacks as growth moments

I do this well	I do this OK	I rarely do this	I don't do this or never thought to do it	N/A
4	3	2	1	0

59. Forgive others

I do this well	I do this OK	I rarely do this	I don't do this or never thought to do it	N/A
4	3	2	1	0

60. Read books that you enjoy

I do this well	I do this OK	I rarely do this	I don't do this or never thought to do it	N/A
4	3	2	1	0

61. Cultivate interest

I do this well	I do this OK	I rarely do this	I don't do this or never thought to do it	N/A
4	3	2	1	0

62. Make time for self-reflection

I do this well	I do this OK	I rarely do this	I don't do this or never thought to do it	N/A
4	3	2	1	0

Tally your score below.

I do this well	I do this OK	I rarely do this	I don't do this or never thought to do it	N/A
4pts	3pts	2pts	1pts	0pts
			Total Points	

248-200-Above Average -Mastery

199-125-Average -Intermediate

124-62-Below Average- Basic

61-0-Severly Below Average -Beginner

Congratulation

Congratulations and Thank You for taking the Hustle Culture Personal and Professional Development Readiness Assessment. It is my hope that through this assessment you were able to reflect and evaluate your personal and workforce readiness.

If you scored below mastery don't get frustrated. Hustle Culture is an everyday journey. We all have areas in our life that we must improve. So, stay positive and keep going because the Hustle never stops.

I am very proud of you. You made it this far in your journey to develop a blueprint to transform your life. You have taken a giant leap of faith that you won't regret.

Because of that leap of faith. I want to do something special for you! Because you have both the Hustle Culture Book and Workbook and have taken the assessment; I am going to give you an opportunity to have a life coaching and assessment analysis! That's right for a limited time, you can receive a free life coaching session.

While I was working on final draft of Hustle Culture, I was able to develop a strategic partnership with Goal Line Coaching. Goal Line Coaching is a national certified, life coaching company that was created as a direct response to the overwhelming need for people to discover their own Personal Playbook.

Over the years, I have seen countless people, regardless of age, gender, and ethnic background, strive to become their best self: but they are unable to run the right plays that will lead to success. What I have found is that sometimes the missing link between them and running the right play, is having a great coach.

I want you to run the right play from now on and live an Unlimited life. That is why I felt that this partnership was needed. All you have to do is visit WWW.GOALLINECOACHINGCO.COM and select Hustle Culture Assessment.

Check out using the code HCULTURE21 and you receive a $200.00 assessment and coaching session for free.

I have provided more information in the resource section of this book. Once again thank you! I am honored to be with you on this Hustle Culture Journey.

Section IX-Resources

GOAL LINE COACHING
CROSS YOUR FINISH LINE ONE CHAT AT A TIME

Because everyone needs their own personal PLAYBOOK!

Life can be challenging at times, even for those among us who seemingly have it all together. Goal Line Coaching understands that these moments are not designed for us to quit in despair; but instead, these are growing moments and opportunities for self-discovery, and clarity. Welcome to Goal Line Coaching where we help you discover your Personal Playbook and help you cross your personal finish line one chat at a time.

One on One Coaching
Take the time to invest in yourself and develop a plan that will make your life thrive. We will help you create and implement a personal plan to create the life you want!

Group Coaching
Join one of our small coaching groups! Each of these power groups are completely different & cover topics from relationships to personal development.

Sister Huddle
Sister Huddle is a collection of podcasts, blogs, individual and group coaching sessions, mentoring and events that are designed to transform the lives of women.

Clients choose us!

We are the best at helping people reach their goals. We specialize in connectivity, personalization, and accountability. We are nationally certified and professional life coaches.

6809 Main Street Unit #21, Cincinnati snperkins@gpunltd.com www.goallinecochingco.com

Book	Author	Category
The Attention Revolution	Alan Wallace	Stress-management Mediation Personal Development
Business Adventures: Twelve Classic Tales from the World of Wall Street	John Brooks	Business Motivation
The Intelligent Investor	Benjamin Graham	Stocks Personal Finance
Daring Greatly: How the Courage to Be Vulnerable Transforms the Way We Live, Love, Parent, and Lead	Brené Brown	Personal Development
Eat That Frog! 21 Great Ways to Stop Procrastinating and Get More Done in Less Time	Brian Tracy	Personal Development Time Management Organizational
The Meditations of Marcus Aurelius.	Marcus Aurelius.	Personal Development Leadership Wisdom
So Good They Can't Ignore You	Cal Newport	Personal Development Professional Development
Why Didn't They Teach Me This in School?	Cary Siegel	Personal Development Personal Finance
Blue Ocean Strategy: How To Create Uncontested Market Space And Make The Competition Irrelevant	Chan Kim and Renee Mauborgne	Personal Development
Smarter, Faster, Better	Charles Duhigg	Personal Development Time Management Purpose Thinking
The Power of Habit: Why We Do What We Do in	Charles Duhigg	Personal Development

Life and Business		
Virtual Freedom: How to Work with Virtual Staff to Buy More Time, Become More Productive, and Build Your Dream Business	Chris Ducker	Entrepreneurship
An Astronaut's Guide to Life on Earth: What Going to Space Taught Me About Ingenuity, Determination, and Being Prepared for Anything	Chris Hadfield	Personal Development Professional Development
Dream Big	Cristiane Correa	Entrepreneurship
Mindsight	Daniel J. Siegel	Personal Development Mental Health
Thinking, Fast and Slow	Daniel Kahneman	Mental Health Thinking
Getting Things Done: The Art of Stress-Free Productivity	David Allen	Work-Life Balance Personal Development
The Automatic Millionaire	David Bach	Personal Finance
Feeling Good	David D. Burns	Mental Health
The Magic of Thinking Big	David J. Schwartz	Personal Development
The Power of Positive Thinking	Dr. Norman Vincent Peale	Positive Thinking Personal Development
Influence: The Psychology of Persuasion, Revised Edition	Dr. Robert Cialdini	Influence Persuasion Sales
What to Say When You Talk to Your Self	Dr. Shad Helmstetter	Mental Health
The Power of Now	Eckhart Tolle	Emotional Intelligence Personal Development
Why We Do What We Do: Understanding Self-Motivation	Edward L. Deci	Purpose Goals Personal Development

Broke Millennial: Stop Scraping By and Get Your Financial Life Together"	Erin Lowry	Personal Finance Motivational
Crush It! Why NOW Is the Time to Cash In on Your Passion	Gary Vaynerchuk	Entrepreneurship Ecommerce
Talent is Overrated	Geoff Colvin	Purpose Mission Vision Personal Development
10X Rule	Grant Cardone	Organization Time Megaevent
Secrets of the Millionaire Mind	Harv Eker	Personal Development Financial
The Success Principles	Jack Canfield	Motivation Success
As You Think	James Allen	Thinking Personal Development
Failing Forward	John C. Maxwell	Personal Development
Spark	John Ratey	Fitness Personal Development
The Only Skill That Matters	Jonathan A. Levi	Professional Development
Simplify	Joshua Becker	Minimalization
Philosophy for Life	Jules Evans	Thinking
Love Yourself Like Your Life Depends On	Kamal Ravikant	Personal Development
The Confidence Code: The Science and Art of Self-Assurance	Katty Kay	Personal Development Motivational Confidence
Nice Girls Don't Get the Corner Office: Unconscious Mistakes Women Make That Sabotage Their Careers	Lois P. Frankel	Women Personal Development Success
Outliers The Story of Success	Malcolm Gladwell	Motivational Success Personal Development
Think and Grow Rich-	Napoleon Hill.	Thinking

1937		Personal Development
The Now Habit: A Strategic Program for Overcoming Procrastination and Enjoying Guilt-Free Play	Neil Fiore	Time Management Organization
Long Walk To Freedom	Nelson Mandela	Motivation
The Last Lecture	Randy Pausch	Motivation
Principles	Ray Dalio	Personal Development
Seagull	**Jonathan Livingston**	Motivational
What Color Is Your Parachute? 2016: A Practical Manual for Job-Hunters and Career-Changers	Richard N. Bolles	Personal Development Professional Development
The 48 Laws of Power	Robert Greene	Personal Development
Whatcha Gonna Do with That Duck?	Seth Godin	Personal Development
Lean In: Women, Work, and the Will to Lead	Sheryl Sandberg	Women Personal Development Professional Development.
The 7 Habits of Highly Effective People	Stephen. R. Covey	Time Management
The Money Book for the Young, Fabulous & Broke	Suze Orman	Personal Finance
Stop Acting Rich	Thomas Stanley	Personal Finance
The 4-Hour Workweek: Escape 9-5, Live Anywhere, and Join the New Rich	Timothy Ferriss	Ecommerce Personal Development Professional Development
StrengthsFinder 2.0	Tom Rath	Personal Development
Money: Master the Game	Tony Robbins	Personal Finance
Awaken the Giant Within	Tony Robbins	Personal Development
365 Ways to Live Cheap: Your Everyday Guide to Saving Money	Trent Hamm	Personal Finance
Your Money or Your Life	Vicki Robin	Personal Finance
Man's Search For Meaning	Victor. E. Frankl	Purpose Personal Development

| **Steve Jobs** | Walter Isaacson. | Motivational |

Professional Appearance Answer Key

a. **Which of the following is the best example of professional business dress?**
   - Kelly is wearing a black skirt suit with two-inch heels.

b. **Which of the following is the best example of business casual?**
   - Nyla is wearing jeans with a nice blouse and suit jacket.

c. **Which of the following colors is ARE considered as appropriate for a business dress suit?**
   - green

g. **6-inch heels are appropriate attire for business dress as long as the woman can walk in them comfortably.**
   - False

e. **A proper handshake has which four elements?**
   - clean hands, firm grip, eye contact, smile

f. **How does your professional appearance impact your career?**
   - Your appearance strongly influences other people's perception of your suitability for hire or promotion.

g. **Your clothing should always be stylish and_____.**

   - Functional

Table Etiquette Answer Key:

a. When you have finished eating, place the knife and fork_____.
- On the plate

b. Begin to eat_____.
- When the everyone is served, and the host starts eating.

c. Sit comfortably at the table, with your feet_____.
- On the floor

d. What adds MOST to the enjoyment of a meal?
- Conversation

e. It is proper to_____.
- Chew with your mouth closed

f. When drinking water, hold the glass_____.
- Near the base

g. When you are eating, keep_____.
- The elbows off the table

h. What should you do when food you dislike is served to you?
- Eat what you can and do not eat the food that you dislike

i. When bread is served at the meal_____.
- Cut piece in half and butter it

j. When you have finished eating_____.
- Leave your plate in place

Professionalism Quiz (Answer Key)

A. TRUE/FALSE

___T_ Keeping nails neatly trimmed and clean only applies to women not to men.

__T__ All professionals display professionalism at all times.

B. Multiple Choice

Would any company culture encourage upper-level management to wear Hawaiian shorts and polo shirts to work?

- No

D. Identify 5 examples of successful work propensities.
- **Dependability**
- **Punctuality**
- **Teamwork**
- **Time Management**
- **Organizational Skills**

G & P Unlimited Co.

G & P Unlimited Co is conglomerate of multiple lifestyle Companies and affiliates. We are a multi-industry company and for the past 10 years, we have developed the most exclusive collection of lifestyle brands and services. Our lifestyle brand and service are:

- *G & P Unlimited Co.*
- *Goal Line Coaching*
- *K. A. Perkins*
- *S.N. Perkins*
- *I'ame*
- *Avodah Ministries*
- *Generational Unlimited*
- *Sister Huddle*
- *G & P Quality Homes*
- *Idyllic Parousia*
- *G & P Adventure Co.*
- *Generational Unlimited*
- *Hustle Culture Co.*
- *C.A. Perkins (Affiliate)*
- *Unlimited Innovation*

G & P Unlimited Co. has a strategic advantage as holding conglomerates which include:

- *Savings on media spending*
- *Better accessibility/negotiation*
- *Professional management*
- *Broad range of products and services.*

G & P Unlimited Co. is a close-knit conglomerate who are dedicated to sharing their knowledge and experience though meaningful garments, educational books, inspiring music, and educational courses and more.

G & P Unlimited Co. Mission

G & P Unlimited Co. is Unlimited Lifestyle Company. We promote Hustle mentality and purpose perspective to help you follow your unique path and guide those who are lost or seek assistance. We are always here for people to make sure they live the best life. Our Unlimited Lifestyle brands show that limits exist only in your head.

G& P Unlimited Co. Vision

To be the pioneer of the Unlimited Lifestyle and the leaders in Hustle Culture and Consciousness. To inspire and motivate people to be great in their individual work, worship, and service.

G& P Unlimited Co. Values

Hustle Culture, helping and empowering people are the core values of G & P Unlimited Co. Our success as a company is measured by the success of our customers.

G& P Unlimited Co. Goals

Our Goals at G & P Unlimited Co. are aimed at empowering like-minded people. We offer limitless educational opportunities, books, and music. We inspire to bring Hope and Hustle to the world.

G & P Unlimited Co. Motto

Hope Mentality, a Pursuit Purpose Perspective, and a Hustle Culture. Live Life - Be Unlimited - Become Legendary

G & P Unlimited Co. Tagline

We do it for the Culture! We Hustle for the People!

PoEthics Philosophy

We are committed to being active corporate citizens. Our hallmark work is PoEthics – servant leadership to humanity, outstanding ethical conduct and resolute responsibility to our communities. We believe that service must be entrenched within our ethos, and translated in our Company's culture, to ensure that we are creating an environment that inspires people, both customers and employees, to Live Boldly, to Live Authentically and to Live Unlimited.

Lifestyle Company

Our supporters are activist, artist, blipsters, clergy, civic leaders, educators, entrepreneurs, hipsters, innovators and minimalist who live a life of service to humanity (PoEthics).

Consciousness Culture

We are inspiring supporters to live holistic lives. Our blog and products are centered around helping you to be inspired, motivated, and educated to thrive so when you are in the middle of the Hustle you are performing at your peak.

GNR8N Unlimited

Generation Unlimited Organization was formed to help eradicate the barriers that disadvantaged youth and young adult's encounter. At G & P, we know that while providing information and inspiring books are helpful, it must be coupled with action. For this reason, your continual support of G & P Unlimited Company and Brands will help us provide free services such as shelter, food, counseling, educational resources, social service resources, job readiness resources, and etc.,

http://generationunlimited.com

When You Support Our Company

When you support or make purchases of products and services from G & P Unlimited Co., you are helping us help people. Through your generous support, we can make the online version of books like TIKVAH for free. G & P Unlimited Co. also donates 10% of company profits to our Generation Unlimited Organization.

Attention Vendors

Any person, business, organization, or group can become a distributor of G & P Unlimited products. By simply purchasing a minimum number of 10 books you are entitled to G & P Unlimited Co. the wholesale rate. The discount for our products varies according to the specific product.

To continue to receive ongoing wholesale rates, you must apply and at least purchase $200 worth of G&P Products per quarter.

Distribution Membership Benefits
- *Newsletters*
- *Economic Opportunities*
- *Sample Products*
- *Promotional Pre-Released Books (PDF)*
- *Networking Events*
- *Entrepreneurial Opportunities*

Distribution Membership Requirements
- *Application on File*
- *Purchase at least $200.00 worth of products per quarter (3 months period).*

For more information visit us at www.gpunlimitedco.com or email us at info@gpunltd.com

Become a Facilitator

If you have been changed by our books become an G & P Unlimited Co. Facilitator. This is a two-day intensive program designed to provide you with the skills you need to create powerful, transformative workshops. G & P Unlimited Co. Facilitator training will provide you with the tools you need to enhance your confidence, create new depth to your presentations.

You will learn how to:

- *Create and engaging environment that stimulate discussion.*
- *Lead session that that will leave your participants feeling touched, open, valued, and nurtured.*
- *Generate an environment where women and men communicate more authentically.*
- *Listen profoundly*
- *Create a powerful relatedness with strangers quickly and easily.*
- *Be more open to others and able to give and receive comfortably.*
- *Create strong boundaries for yourself without shutting others down.*

You will also learn:

* *The skills that can be used to sell each of the products while also creating your own stream of income.*
* *How to use the **Advertisement Tool Kit** to Generate Sales or Host Coach Talk Parties*
* *How to set-up a **Successful Influencer and Affiliate** income using our products.*
* *Much More*

For more information about this wonderful opportunity, don't hesitate to contact info@gpunltd.com or visit us online at www.gpunlimitedco.com

About the Author

Highly dedicated, innovative, and goal-driven, K. A. Perkins is a maverick Author, Educator, Consultant, and Influencer whose underlying mission is to deeply empower others to unlock their full potential. As the CEO of G & P Unlimited Co and holding a strong track record of instilling positive self-development transformations, K. A. enjoys every moment of utilizing his creative-eye, past experiences, and rooted passion for guiding others towards becoming the best versions of themselves.

Growing up with humble beginnings, K. A. learned early on the true meaning behind commitment, resilience, and a strong work ethic. These core principles, along with intense perseverance, are what shaped him to overcome disappointments and hardships in life and achieve monumental success. After reaching this balancing point, K. A. chose to fulfill a promise he had made to his younger self, a promise to share the tough lessons he faces during his journey in hopes that valuable information will become the stepping stones for others to learn from and thrive. Not only has K. A. done just that by launching his brand with a fashionable twist, but he is also a loving father and husband who is dedicated to setting a prime example of how a real man is supposed to be through his efforts.

In the end, nothing makes K. A. happier than being able to help others unlock the quality of life and confidence they deserve and influencing a future generation composed of true world changers.

Whether it be via fashion, news, information, events, and media, K. A. has a true ardency for what he does and demonstrated that by developing G & P Unlimited Co on a foundation of authenticity, integrity, and trust and raising the urban streetwear fashion bar. This, in conjunction with his keen artistic nature and reputation promoting self-development that society as a whole can benefit from.

A proud HBCU graduate and member of Alpha Phi Alpha Fraternity Incorporated, K.A. Perkins can give you the solidifying confidence that you have come to the right place to advance your life and style to new prospering levels.

INVITE K.A. PERKINS TO SPEAK TO YOUR NEXT EVENT

If you would like for K.A. Perkins or a member of the G & P Unlimited Team to come speak, please contact us at info@gpunltd.com.

Current Books
- Tikvah

Upcoming Books

- Pearls of Possibility
- The Shift

For More Products and Updates Visit https://gpunltd.com **or** https://kaperkins.com

G & P Unlimited Co.

Hope Mentality, a Pursue Perspective, and a Hustle Culture. -Live Life-Be Unlimited-Become Legendary

www.ingramcontent.com/pod-product-compliance
Lightning Source LLC
Chambersburg PA
CBHW080923180426
43192CB00040B/2667